A Retreat for Everyday Life

Inspired by Ronald Knox

by
Fr Paul Dobson

*All booklets are published thanks to the
generous support of the members of the
Catholic Truth Society*

CATHOLIC TRUTH SOCIETY
PUBLISHERS TO THE HOLY SEE

Contents

Image: Page 55: © National Portrait Gallery, London

All rights reserved. First published 2016 by The Incorporated Catholic Truth Society, 40-46 Harleyford Road London SE11 5AY Tel: 020 7640 0042 Fax: 020 7640 0046. © 2016 The Incorporated Catholic Truth Society.

ISBN 978 1 78469 119 6

How to Use this Booklet

Being the parish priest of a rather large parish, under the patronage of St Isaac Jogues, one of the Canadian Martyrs, just east of Toronto, we have many apostolates and organisations. One is called, Teams of Our Lady (TOOL), whose aim is to assist married couples to live their vocation more faithfully and fruitfully. The members of 'TOOL' asked me, their chaplain, to give them a retreat on a Saturday morning. Wondering what to say, I sought the aid of Monsignor Ronald Knox, whose insights into the faith and common sense I have long admired. So, I re-read his book, *Retreat for Lay People*, for edification and inspiration, and was able to extract some good material for the gathering of the couples on retreat. From that retreat, this booklet was born.

The booklet is divided into three parts: Part One: Foundations; Part Two: The Life and Death of Our Blessed Lord; Part Three: Practical Day-to-Day Needs.

This booklet, I hope, can be used as a source of sound information for anyone, priest or otherwise, called upon to lead a retreat for the lay faithful. If you are unable, for whatever reason, to have a guided retreat you may wish to use this booklet over a weekend, beginning on Friday evening and ending on Sunday, following the three parts. Alternatively, you may wish to read the booklet straight through in one sitting, over a period of twenty four days or indeed any one or more of the sections whose subject matter appeals to you. The choice is entirely yours.

At the end of each part, Knox made suggested resolutions for those who are following the devotion of the Holy Hour and I saw no reason to omit this worthy inclusion.

Introduction

"Where are you?" (Gn 3:9)

The first question God asks us is: "Where are you?" in the third chapter of the book of *Genesis*. This searching question is always a good one to ask oneself, particularly during a retreat or in a thorough examination of conscience. While it is true that God is hidden from us in so many ways, we are not to hide ourselves from God. We need, from time to time, to spend a concentrated time in retreat from the business of our normal routine to be with God, to be in conversation with him.

Some months ago, I was in New York City and, while I enjoy this extraordinary place and what it has to offer, I was conscious of just how noisy it was: the drills, the sirens, the music, the chatter. I can honestly say that my senses were overstimulated. It has been said that we live in an Age of Feeling, and I felt exhausted by the clamour of New York. Hence, the need to go on a retreat: to rest, to be quiet, to move from the many gifts of the world and look to the Giver. To this end, we have Monsignor Ronald Knox (1888-1957) to serve as a guide. One of Knox's last books was *A Retreat for Lay People* and his most popular. The twenty four meditations fall into three groups of eight: the first represents the foundations, the second is based on the life and death of Christ and the third envisages practical day-to-day needs.

While Knox says that it is difficult to find the perfect book on retreat I see his retreat material as a generous offering to suit a wide variety of palates. Knox says that "there is a daintiness in your spiritual tastes which calls for the meal *à la carte* rather than the *table d'hôte*." I trust you'll find this to be the case with what Knox provides as a fruit of his faith in the Lord, as well as his keen insights and humour.

Part One:
Foundations

▶ 1. Discouragement in Retreat

> *"Do not let your hearts be troubled; trust in God still and trust in me."* (Jn 14:1)

The Gospels tell us curiously little about the "machinery", as Knox calls it, of Our Lord's life on earth, for instance, the houses he actually lived in, the rooms he took his meals in. We are left with a remarkable sense of mystery and this mystery, while beautiful and real, can leave us bewildered. This is how we may feel at the start of a retreat: bewildered and even overwhelmed by the mystery of faith before us. Our life with the Lord is rightly understood as a pilgrimage, and thus on the way, we tire: our feet get sore, we are thirsty and we want to reach our destination quickly. We may even be bored rigid and wonder what's the point of it all?

Knox in speaking of ordinary Christians says that regarding the practice of our religion, we experience a sense of staleness. And this comes from a defect in ourselves, which is a natural defect. Even the experience of a great love disappoints us, and no marriage can be a perpetual honeymoon. Knox reminds us sensibly not to expect too much of a sensational experience in retreat. "No, try to hold yourself steadily and humbly in the presence of God, telling him it's his will you should be making this effort, and there must be something he means his Holy Spirit to do in you; you are content to lie fallow, and let the seed strike."

A beautiful prayer to God the Holy Spirit concludes this section which I encourage you to use throughout this retreat and as often as you see fit: *Come, Holy Spirit, not with outward manifestations, not with tongues of fire, but silently, as the warmth of spring creeps into the barren earth; come to this cenacle of a human heart, and stir the dull airs of it with the breath of hope.*

Suggested resolution: to say with the psalmist "I delight to do thy will, O Lord." (*Ps* 40)

▶ 2. Alive to God

"I have come so that they may have life and have it to the full." (*Jn* 10:10)

"To God, all things are alive; O come, let us adore him." These words from Matins of the Dead form the focus of this reflection. Nothing can exist away from God. As the flowers open to the sun from which they receive their vigour, so in the natural and supernatural order all things turn continually before God, who is their sun. We look to Christ, the very Word of God, whose every word is creative. Our Lord knows how to calm us: "Peace, be still." And there is a dead hush instantly.

In life we need to distinguish between living and being alive. We can say we are living even if we are drunk or in a state of mortal sin, but are we truly alive to God? Being alive to God means more than mere respiration, mere circulation of the blood. "And when we talk of the Christian life we mean, please God, something more than *not* being in mortal sin. We mean a kind of spiritual vitality, however feeble, however fitful," Knox reminds us. This is in contrast to the selfish person, says Knox, who "concentrates his whole attention…on the things which minister to his own contentment or amuse or attract him." And this, in turn, is in contrast to the one who is alive to God; it means that the thought of God is at the very "apex" of our unconscious minds all the time, overflowing into our thoughts and acts. It is "like a taste in the mouth, a perfume in the nostrils…" It is like being "haunted by the Divine Presence."

Turning to a domestic scene, without wanting to be undignified, Knox uses the image of the attitude of a dog towards its master, an attitude which you may describe as one of "habitual attention". In our resolution to being "alive to God" Knox recommends that we "shut down", just for a minute or two, the busy distractions and go to God. He calls it a minute or two "stolen for God", when you find yourself waiting for a bus, or left with nothing to do while the kettle boils.

Finally, Knox recommends that we make a deliberate gesture of freedom to God, by throwing out both arms, rather like the gesture you make after a "heavy meal or when you are feeling sleepy." You throw out your arms, as it were, towards Almighty God "reminding yourself that you are alive, alive to him; that you are awake, and ready to listen."

> **Suggested resolution:** to thank God at the end of the day or week for the many ways he has shown his care and actually count his blessings.

▶ 3. Today

"Every day, as long as this 'today' lasts, keep encouraging one another so that no one is hardened by the lure of sin". (*Heb* 3:13)

From the *Epistle to the Hebrews* these words are recorded: "Every day, as long as this 'today' lasts, keep encouraging one another so that no one is hardened by the lure of sin." So let us meditate on that single word "Today". God has given us, for the ordering of our lives, an alternation of day and night. Each day is separated by "a thick black line of oblivion." Each morning is a fresh start for us, a kind of re-birth and so it is good when we wake from sleep to offer our day to God. The traditional Morning Offering is a commendable practice in this regard. Even if we cannot make it every day to the Holy Sacrifice of the Mass, we can be in union with Christ who offers himself anew for us each day on the altars throughout the world.

The Holy Spirit himself urges us: "If today you hear his voice, harden not your hearts." And so we need to listen to the voice of God. He speaks to us in a whisper as he spoke to Elias. We listen to him in our hearts and in the silence of our conscience. Knox says: "Get back into the habit of recollection, and the resolutions will come to you, afterwards in disguise."

Knox refers us to a master of the spiritual life, Père de Caussade, on the importance of the sacrament of the present moment. This is the most useful of all shortcuts to perfection: the job you're doing at the present moment, if it is your job, is quite certainly God's will for you. In whatever work we're doing, let us ask for no more than the grace to avoid those sins, says Knox, which lie between "bed-time and bed-time." Let us make today a holiday even from our venial sins, we are instructed.

St Gertrude reminds us to look to nature, to the early morning, and bids us to pay attention to the newness of things. We ought to offer our hearts to God every morning as a rose with the dew still on it. Think of the freshness, do not rob it of its innocence. "We will not give in our names to that human conspiracy of sin!"

On this day, we will accept God's gifts of food and leisure and recreation lovingly, yet careful not to let them get the better of us. Sometimes at funerals I remind the mourners of the conclusion of the Hail Mary, in which we implore Our Lady to pray for us at the two most important moments of our life (the two nows): "now and at the hour of our death."

Knox concludes by referring to Our Lord's absolution of the Good Thief: "And from that Heart, busy with all the tragedies of a universe came, today thou shalt be with me in paradise."

Suggested resolution: upon waking each day, to make a prayer of self-offering to God, uniting yourself intentionally with him.

▶ 4. The Fear of Death

"Death is swallowed up in victory. Death, where is your victory? Death, where is your sting? The sting of death is sin, and sin gets its power from the law. So let us thank God, for giving us the victory through Our Lord Jesus Christ." (1 Co 15:54-56)

The thought of death takes some effort. We fear the thought because death is painful, the separation of the soul from the body which are created and meant to be together. To be in a disembodied state, however temporary, is a kind of violation. We still await the resurrection of the body at the end of time, as we say in the Creed. The thought of death puts things into perspective: our life here on earth is only a preface for eternal life. Knox provides this image: we should think of ourselves as soldiers on sentry duty, ready to be relieved by our Commanding Officer at a time of his own choosing. The thought of death is good for us, too, because it prevents us from getting too wrapped up in this world, and the goods of this world; shrouds have no pockets, we are soberly reminded.

Pope Francis, has pointed this out in his apostolic exhortation, *The Joy of the Gospel*, amongst other places, that "reality is greater than ideas." And death is one of the great realities, indeed one of the the Four Last Things. Knox again provides a beautiful thought on this most real of realities: death is a "transition from a world of shadows to a world of realities, this carriage he graciously sends to fetch us, when he wants us to come and join him." We die many times before the ultimate death: death to school (when we graduate), one week dies to make room for another, winter gives way for spring and so on. All of these 'small deaths' are a kind of preparation for the final curtain call.

Knox tells us a story of Archbishop Goodier, who gave him his ordination retreat. The archbishop said that it was a good thing to pray for the kind of death that appealed to you. It was surprising, he said, how often one finds that particular prayer granted. In the case of the archbishop, Knox wonders if he prayed for a sudden death because "he didn't like the idea of the bottles." A priest went to call on him one day at Teignmouth, and the archbishop saw him off at the door. When he got a little away, he saw the door still standing open so he went back and found the archbishop just inside, dead.

We turn our thoughts again to Holy Mass, the Sacrifice of sacrifices, on which our life should be centred. The crucial moment in the Holy Mass is when the priest says:

Hoc est enim Corpus meum. And in death we too should echo these words: "This is my body, the body thou gavest me, and art now taking away from me. Let us be ready to make this supreme confession of our creatureliness." Knox gives us a little prayer that turns our minds to the importance of a good and holy death: *Come, holy oils, and seal these gateways of sense, the points of contact in me between body and soul; seal them well, this is a secret present from me to my God.*

Suggested resolution: to pray for the kind of death that appeals to you in the hour the Lord appoints.

▶ 5. Watching

"And what I say to you I say to all: stay awake!" (*Mk* 13:37)

God watches, while man sleeps. However, it is a rhetorical convention in the Old Testament, in the psalms particularly, to complain that the Almighty God has gone to sleep. Pope Benedict XVI in one of his talks said that our prayer awakens God when he *appears* to be asleep. The Church in all her members, Head and Body, continues to pray, even and especially when the stormed-tossed boat, as an image of the Church, seems to be sinking.

The saints, the masterpieces of God's handiwork, provide many examples of heartfelt prayer from St Paul to St Patrick who got through the whole psalter every night in a vigil of prayer. Our Lord himself speaking of the End Times, in apocalyptic terms, provides this imperative: "And what I say to you I say to all: stay awake!"

Knox reminds us of the artistic rendering of the Eye of God, over the chancel arch in some churches that was looking at us all the time. Cardinal Basil Hume in his book, *The Mystery of the Incarnation*, gives an interpretation of the Watchful Eye of God:

A little boy was taken to visit an old lady. The old lady pointed out to him a text on her wall: "Thou, God, seest me." She said to him: "You see those words? They do not mean that God is always watching you to see what you are doing wrong. They mean that he loves you so much that he cannot take his eyes off you." Hume ends the story by saying: "We have to keep our eyes on him."

> **Suggested resolution:** to look at the crucifix and make an act of faith, hope and love.

▶ 6. The World to Come

"Now as he blessed them, he withdrew from them and was carried up to heaven. They worshipped him". (*Lk* 24:51-52)

While it is true that God has made us for eternal life, and desires us for the life of glory, it is important for the believer not to "play with the Divine Mercy". We must not take our eternal salvation for granted as if we were simply on an assembly line, a great conveyor belt, that ushers us into heaven after our earthly lives are over. Many get so caught up in day-to-day life that they forget about God. So perfect is the illusion of security all around us that they forget they are forgetting him, emphasises Knox.

As God is not a puppeteer, but our Merciful Father who desires our attention, he allows us to forget about him, if we insist on it. The unseen power of God maintains such a person in existence; he exists but he does not live. He is like a clock without hands; he has lost his whole reason for existing, Knox says.

In one of his many magnificent sermons St Augustine defined atheism as "forgetfulness". The antidote to this is to remember who made us (that we didn't make ourselves and mercifully, no one voted us into existence) and why it is that we were made to begin with, as the first two questions of the old Penny Catechism highlight. Returning to the same catechism we find the wonderful definition of prayer that allows us to keep God always at the centre of our lives: "Prayer is the raising of the mind and heart to God." May this be so today and every day.

Suggested resolution: to pray right now and say: "Let me never forget you, O Lord."

► 7. The Spirit of Faith

"I, the light, have come into the world, so that whoever believes in me need not stay in the dark any more." (Jn 12:46)

Knox doesn't speak here of the theology of faith but as it is found in real life, linked to love and truth. The truth of which he is speaking is not a set of abstract propositions, however august. We are to love the truth as it is in Christ; he himself is Truth Incarnate, Love Incarnate too. To speak the truth and love what is true is to stay close to Christ. In this way, the life of faith is something relational and social.

The words of Pope Benedict XVI from his first encyclical, *Deus Caritas Est* are fitting conclusion: "Being Christian is not the result of an ethical choice or a lofty idea, but the encounter with an event, a person, which gives life a new horizon and a decisive direction." Let this guide you as we continue on in our retreat and daily life in deepened friendship with Christ the Lord.

Suggested resolution: to speak the truth in love even when it is not convenient.

► **8. The Love of God**

"The love of God has been poured into our hearts by the Holy Spirit which has been given us." (Rm 5:5)

The love of God is a frightening topic for Knox not because he doubts God's love for his creatures, but rather he doubts our love for God. Our whole reason for being in the world is to love God - all the saints, all the pious books agree on this point. Additionally, it is a commandment. In fact, it is *the* commandment and Knox reminds us that loving God gives you "an appetite for loving your neighbour, just as taking a walk gives you an appetite for your food."

Knox is well acquainted with the biblical languages and he reminds us that in the Old Testament if we look how often it refers to loving God, you'll find only thirty-three quotations, and a dozen of them from *Deuteronomy*. Nearly all the Old Testament is about fearing God or seeking him. But for us Christians, loving "is *the* thing; it's what we're here for." God has provided us with this commandment because we are inconstant in our love. When our wills are weak, we are reminded by the wisdom found in the commandments which come from the Heart of God.

If we are poor lovers of God, and I suspect no one would say he or she wasn't, we can look to St Augustine for guidance to see ourselves in a different light. This extraordinary Doctor of the Church said that we are all of us beggars, standing cap in hand at the front door of the great Householder, Almighty God.

Knox remarks: "He wants us to stand there, like sturdy beggars, and say, 'Excuse me, I know it sounds like a silly thing to say, but I haven't got any love. I'm right out of it!'" Or turning to the great saint of joy, St Philip Neri, who never tired of saying: "My God, I don't love you one bit!"

Our final thought is taken from Pope Benedict's luminous encyclical on love: "Love is indeed 'ecstasy', not in the sense of a moment of intoxication, but rather as a journey, an ongoing exodus out of the closed inward-looking self towards its liberation through self-giving, and thus towards authentic self-discovery and indeed the discovery of God."

> **Suggested resolution:** since love is the 'exodus of the self' what simple word or gesture shall I make today or tomorrow that will make me 'exit' myself in a clear and concrete way?

Part Two:

The Life and Death of Our Blessed Lord

Holy Hour - A Hidden God

God is hidden in four ways: in creation, in his dealings with men, by the Incarnation and in the Holy Eucharist.

Creation: God hides or rather reveals himself in creation. We, Knox says, have a dreadful power of refusing to think, often being distracted and enslaved by creation. We see the robe God wears and not himself. God plays a kind of hide and seek with us in creation. Why, we might wonder? Knox says in order to challenge us, to cost us something. We do not value things if they don't cost us something.

One Jesuit retreat master I once heard said that God likes a good story and as a result does not always make himself so obvious. Instead, he awaits our search.

Genesis says that God walked in the cool of the afternoon. In consideration of this, St Francis de Sales said that this is the best time for interior prayer, to keep in contact with the Lord God.

Dealings with men: throughout history so many individuals and institutions have appeared successful and then have ended their so-called ascent rather rapidly. Why? To make us aware how we must place our life and trust in God who does not shift and fall with the changing times.

As the psalmist reminds us: "Put not your trust in princes." God hides so that we may learn to give up our own wills, to his holy will, knowing that it is best.

Incarnation: God becomes small and weak in the Christ child. He needs to be fed, to be protected in his Sacred Infancy. Why is this the case? Clearly, so that we might learn to annihilate ourselves, to learn our smallness, to die to ourselves so that he may live in us.

The Holy Eucharist: after the words of consecration, Christ is present sacramentally in his Body and Blood, veiled under the humble appearance of bread and wine. He puts himself in the priests' hands. Our Lord continues his presence among us in the tabernacle, desiring our company. He places himself at our disposal, to worship. We are to put ourselves in his service and take him into the world for the sanctification of many.

▶ 9. Our Lord and the Rich Young Man

"Good master, what must I do to inherit eternal life?" (Mk 10:17)

Our Lord himself knew the feeling of disappointment. We can think of how difficult it must have been for him to see the arguments of his apostles, their power struggles, the betrayal of St Peter, to say nothing of Judas Iscariot.

Knox says that of all the pictures in the Gospels which represent Our Lord as thwarted in his human contacts, none is more poignant than the account given in St Mark of the rich young man. Our Lord gazed on the young man with love and said: "Go and sell all that thou hast, and give to the poor." The young man went away sorrowing, for he had great possessions. "Looked at and loved by the Saviour of the world, and he turns out a failure."

What lessons can we extract from this? First, disappointment was hallowed by Our Lord. What happened to Christ, our forerunner and pattern, will inevitably happen to us. We are therefore in the best of company when failure visits us. Second, when we are betrayed and hurt, fear not, for consolation is always around the corner. Life is a great teacher and we do see in our lives this continual movement from desolation to consolation so clearly emphasised in Ignatian spirituality, among others. Third, our natures are given to us. We are men and women, not machines, and so we cannot simply programme life to turn out as we wish. There is no magic button to press, in order to re-boot in a mechanistic manner. Rather, in union with the mind and heart of Christ, we must respond to life's ups and downs with charity and truth, with the humanity and heavenly graces we have received from a Provident and Merciful Father.

Suggested resolution: to thank God that I am made in his image and not created to imitate someone else.

► 10. Our Lord's Disregard for Appearances

"Man looks at appearances, but the Lord looks at the heart." (1 S 16:7)

We think of Our Lord's life in two parts: private and public. Knox points out that we shouldn't press the point too strictly. Our Lord was always in the public eye, he says. However, he never sought for reputation. When men spoke ill of him, he was content for his Father's love. We, on the other hand, are curious: we usually think we're right, even in the face of mounting evidence to the contrary. We are not infrequently wounded when others don't agree with us. We care desperately what others think. "I do not look for honour from men," Our Lord states. The Lord Jesus, says Knox, had no public relations officer to make good his position before the world.

Keeping up appearances was, in no small way, characteristic of his own people, as well as the human race at large, and undoubtedly of you and me. Think of the emphasis on cleaning the outside of the cup and dish while inside, it's dirty. Our Lord's method, however, saves us from the inside out, from the purification of the heart firstly.

Moving well on from Biblical times, Knox recounts a story of Dr Johnson, the eminent and prolific English writer. When a lady asked him how he came to make some mistake in his dictionary, he replied: "Ignorance, Madam, stark ignorance." You and I haven't, commonly, the honesty to say that. Often we would defend ourselves and shift the blame. All too often we live our lives superficially.

Returning to the Holy Bible: "My eyes are ever fixed on the Lord," wrote King David, and we would like ours to be. Yet instead, Knox says, "we are always looking around at one another, like school-girls in church."

We see again in the life of Our Lord that he was largely silent during his trial and throughout his sacred Passion. Here, as in many other circumstances, the disciple is not above the Master! To do otherwise, to fortify ourselves in human opinion, is a kind of "constructive idolatry".

Knox concludes this important meditation with the following sober words: "It is from…his kindly judgement that we look for that final verdict of 'Well done', which will make all earth's praise look so foolish, and all earth's prizes so trumpery."

Suggested resolution: to say the Our Father, slowly and lovingly, recalling that you are addressing our Heavenly Father, who made us, for eternal life.

▶ **11. Six Steps to the Crucifix**

"They will look on the one whom they have pierced." (Jn 19:37)

Our Lord Jesus Christ entered his Passion and death almost in silence. Not infrequently do we consider silence to be a threat or somehow or other unfriendly in our chatty and noisy world. But how eloquent is Our Lord's silence. His resignation to his Father's will is the answer he communicates for our redemption and sanctification. Our Lord does give a few cryptic answers before Pilate, not likely "to do his cause any good".

On the cross itself, he spoke seven times, but with what economy, Knox reminds us: twenty-eight words, perhaps, in Aramaic. "Almost throughout that tragedy, the chief Actor plays his part in dumb show."

Knox offers six different levels from which we can look at Our Lord's Passion as spectators on Calvary. The crucifix stands on a "plane too high for our intelligence". So let us instead climb the steps, six in number, and kiss each one. The response to this mystery, like all divine mysteries, is to adore.

Step 1: The spectator will look on Calvary and simply see it as the "way of the world". Earlier, in a different but similar way, Socrates was put to death for making people *think* that there is a right and a wrong way of living. Jesus in his turn taught the people the ways of God: "what mattered was the inside of things, being merciful to your neighbour, judging him charitably, trusting Providence, being sorry when you had done wrong." And he was crucified. It is the way of the world.

Step 2: Worldliness: we are sometimes so immersed in the world that we forget who made it and why. The moment, Knox says, we take our eyes off the crucifix, we begin to make the mistake of thinking it's the outside of things which matter. All of us in various ways forget to move beyond the superficial. How anxious we are to explain away our failures. Men loved darkness, rather than the light; "we are truth-shy", all of us, Gentiles as well as Jews. "That is how Socrates came to his end; that is how Jesus of Nazareth came to his end." On this platform, we see the crucifixion "as the defeat of Truth in a world that loves its comfortable evasions." The question is whether we are going to treat it as inevitable or whether we shall try ourselves to do something about it.

Step 3: Christ's violent death draws others in. As he died doing something good, his memory becomes a talisman. "Jesus of Nazareth claims homage, even from millions of people, who do not believe he was God, because his death sealed, unmistakably, the life he had lived." Lifted up, Our Lord draws men to him with a magnetism which cannot be neutralised. "Buried in the ground, this grain of wheat will take life and flourish anew."

Step 4: Christ died so that others might live. Christ is our Divine Friend, and being so, he desires to save his friends.

Step 5: Jesus of Nazareth was not merely crucified for others, but for the sins of others. Where shall we find a parallel to this? A debt was paid by God-made-man.

Step 6: Finally, Knox says that if we only see this death in terms of a debt incurred and a debt paid it remains a little "mathematical". It may appeal to the theologian in us, but it does not "satisfy our hearts". In this mystery of Christ's suffering, we witness the great lengths to which Our Lord goes: suffering, Knox, states, "is the native language of love". Our Lord, concludes Knox, does not want us to understand in some exhaustive sense, he wants us to believe.

> **Suggested resolution:** to venerate the crucifix in your home and learn the Prayer before a Crucifix.

▶ 12. The Passion as Our Lord Saw It

"I have been crucified with Christ, and I live now not with my own life but with the life of Christ who lives in me." (Ga 2:19-20)

A person, as a rule, does not go through a retreat without meditating on Our Lord's Passion. While on retreat or in a period of recollection we tend to think of ourselves. Knox states: "You ask why God made *you*; you reflect on the shortness of life, the vocation God has for *you* in the world, and so on - it is all about *you*." The problem is that we sink into ourselves.

I read a short story in a newspaper recently that illustrates this point rather well of a woman who sunk into herself: "In my twenties, just as full of self-pity and terror as this new generation, I once dropped in to see a priest, Father Fudge, and poured out my woes, imagining he would be both sympathetic and impressed by my torment. Fr Fudge listened quietly, then said: 'The point of being a Christian is not to feel better, it is so God can use you to serve others.' Others? They hadn't occurred to me for a while. I said goodbye to Fr Fudge, feeling not triggered or marginalised but unaccountably lighter. It wasn't all about me! I actually laughed with the relief of it."

This is the point. We must 'zoom out' and look beyond ourselves, look to the One whose estimation really matters. Let us see things, Knox says, through the eye of the Saviour: go higher, aim higher.

Knox urges us to enter into a form of meditation known as "composition of place": to put ourselves in the drama of the Passion. Therefore, do take up one of the Passion accounts and read it with care or have someone read parts to you and then why not pray together? What sounds do you hear? What do you see? What are you thinking and feeling? What manageable resolutions will you make?

Knox concludes this chapter by saying the following: "We have been trying to put ourselves in the Heart of Jesus Christ. Let us ask God to put Jesus Christ into your heart and mine, so that it may be Christ living in us, as long as we live, Christ dying in us, when we come to die."

Suggested resolution: to read one of the Passion accounts.

▶ 13. The Problem of Suffering

"I am the Good Shepherd. The Good Shepherd is the one who lays down his life for his sheep." (Jn 10:11)

Isaiah foretells most clearly Our Lord's Passion and death. We hear the account every Good Friday during the Sacred Liturgy. Christ was offered on the altar of the cross because he willed it. Knox said that there is one Accomplice who co-operated more effectively with the plans of Our Lord's persecutors than any other, and that is Our Lord himself. There is only one explanation for it: "He wants to die." Because God is infinite there were an infinite number of ways God in Christ could have redeemed us. He could have accomplished the salvation of the world even if he had seen fit to ascend to his Father from his cradle in Bethlehem. Instead, he would taste death, and the indignities which came before. Christ was not content merely to make atonement, he would make it in full.

What was the meaning of that? Our Lord is teaching us generosity in the extreme. Christ Jesus is our Saviour first and foremost, yes, our Ransom. He would also be our model.

Suffering, Knox says, winnows the chaff from the wheat, shows up false devotion that is merely "cupboard-love" and makes true devotion shine all the brighter, like gold in the furnace. Christ enters into the world and with love transforms suffering. He gives it meaning. He brings us God. This thought was re-echoed by Pope Benedict XVI in the first volume of his masterful work, *Jesus of Nazareth*:

> The great question that will be with us throughout this entire book: what did Jesus actually bring, if not world peace, universal prosperity, and a better world? What has he brought? The answer is very simple: God. He has brought God…and now we know his face, now we can call upon him. Now we know the path that we human beings have to take in this world. Jesus has brought us God and with God the truth about our origin and destiny: faith, hope and love.

And the Church, Christ's Mystical Body on earth, continues the saving work of the Lord. This is why we have the treasure that is the sacraments and the reason for the Church's pastoral care for the suffering in any situation and circumstance: to bring God to those in need. Whatever our suffering, "let us unite it with Our Lord's Agony and Passion, thanking him that he has deigned so to take us into his own fellowship, so to honour us with the royal dignity of his cross."

Suggested resolution: to consider what you have learnt from some suffering you have endured and thank the Lord for his Divine Presence and assistance.

▶ 14. The Way of Love

> *"This is my commandment: love one another, as I
> have loved you."* (Jn 15:12)

Our Lord's way is of the cross, the sign of God's unfathomable love. Without it, the Church risks becoming, as Pope Francis is wont to say, an NGO (Non-Governmental Organisation).

I remember in one of my former parishes a father of a family telling the story of his two sons who were playing a game with their toys. One brother said to the other: "I love this toy," to which the other responded: "Do you love it so much that you'd die for it?" This told me that the boys' parents were doing a fine job in communicating the faith, in giving them the content of the faith and a language with which to communicate the same.

Our Blessed Lord who was born of a carpenter's wife will be a carpenter to the end; he does not shrink from shouldering the cross. Even at the last he reaches out to Dismas, who turned to God in his agony and was duly received into paradise.

Our Lord lived the Beatitudes he first taught, as do the many saints down through the ages. Who comes to mind now? The Beatitudes have been called the Charter of the Saints. They are beautiful expressions of how to live the gospel. They are most exacting and seem, Knox says, to ask more of us than what was asked of the children of Israel living under the Old Dispensation. Why is Our Lord asking more of us than he asked of those who went before? It is, Knox tells us, as if Our Lord is saying: "But I am legislating for the children of the gospel, and the children of the gospel will not need this series of prohibitions because they will not want to do harm. They will not need laws telling them not to murder people, because the very emotion of hatred will find no lodging, or no fixed lodging in their hearts." Again, "no need to caution them against adultery, because they will love purity."

Knox sets high the bar when he states: he needs no danger posts who walks steadily in the way of love. Are we not called by God to live in the manner and according to the style of his Divine Son? During this retreat, ask Our Lord to teach us anew the way of love.

Suggested resolution: to realise in a new way that I do not graduate from the Lord's School of Love.

▶ 15. Death as Achievement

"Whereas the sensible ones took flasks of oil as well as their lamps." (*Mt* 25:4)

Knox knew first hand the horrors of war, performing his sacred duties until light began to filter back, slowly and fitfully in 1945. During World War II, Knox was chaplain to a girls' school evacuated from London to Shropshire. He preached to those fortunate girls every

Sunday. And his series of sermons were eventually collected into a volume called *The Mass in Slow Motion* (the parts of the Mass explained step by step). Later, a companion volume appeared called *The Creed in Slow Motion*, and lastly to complete the trilogy some time later, *The Gospel in Slow Motion*. In each volume, he never abandons the conversational tone and he interweaves the most trifling elements in his hearers' lives with the profoundest spirituality quite fascinatingly. Try to obtain these works if you can. If more people read such books, and lived their teachings, peace might have more of a fighting chance, first in our hearts and then outwards.

War, Knox says, is the "last desperate remedy we invoke when the world's politics have grown so tangled that there is no unravelling the knots by any other means." Our Lord, the Prince of Peace, does not settle conflict through a political act. He is not content with short-term solutions. He is interested in and involved with each person, that was, is and ever shall be, in their totality, for the good of their soul here and hereafter. Perhaps this is why Pope Francis once said that the one dogma he is sure of is that "God never gives up on anyone." If we co-operate with God, his kingdom will advance in our weary world.

For our part, most of us will not die as a result of war, but will die all the same. Most of us shall die as we have lived, in an intentional union with God or not. Knox says: "The only history that matters is the history of the individual soul, your soul or mine, working out its eternal salvation." In the end, we are told by this wise monsignor, "the supreme sacrifice which the creature makes to its Creator is the act of dying…to be nothing, and let him be everything."

Let us pray for a good and holy death, fortified by the rites of our Holy Mother, the Church. Spiritual authors are agreed on this urgent and important matter: what needs to concern us is not a sudden death, but a sudden and *unprepared* death! We are to have "oil in our lamps", ready for the return of the Bridegroom.

Suggested resolution: to make a good examination of conscience and go to Confession soon.

▶ 16. The Entombment

"Come and see the place where he lay." (*Mt* 28:6)

Knox bids us to look upon Our Lord taken down from the cross through the eyes of Our Lady. She who bore him in her virginal womb, whose Divine Heart was formed beneath her Immaculate Heart. This is why it is typical to see the images of the Holy Hearts side by side. Knox describes Our Lady as a ciborium used at Holy Mass. This precious vessel eludes notice because of the far more Precious Thing which it contains. It is fitting to look at Our Lord's suffering through the eyes of Our Lady. Who on earth was closer to him than her from the moment of his Incarnation? Our Blessed Lord received his human nature from her. Let us be penetrated by her sentiments of tenderness. She will be there, please God, to help us when we die, to help us on the other side of death; we are her children too.

There is a story of an Irish lady who was accused of paying too much attention to Our Lady, to the neglect of Christ her Son. Her response to this sad accusation was simple and to the the point: "If all Our Lord can say to me on the day of my particular judgement is: 'You paid too much attention to my Mother in your earthly life,' I shan't be too worried."

One of the more famous and splendid artistic images of Our Lady and her Son can be seen in St Peter's Basilica, Rome: the Pieta. She makes a gesture of love, offering to God what, or rather, who she received, while keeping her gaze fixed on him. This is a profound image reflecting what our pilgrimage of faith looks like ideally. We do not have to create the faith or stage manage it or dress it up as a commodity. Rather the role of the believer, as Pope Benedict XVI pointed out in *Jesus of Nazareth*, is to *receive* the faith and *transmit* it, full stop. This is liberating to know and to do, freeing us from the snares of invention and re-invention, over and over again.

One day, Knox reminds us, our bodies too will lie motionless in the arms of the Church, that other kindly mother who has a place and a plan for everyone and everything. In 2009, my own father, Paul, died and I had the privilege to offer Holy Mass for the repose of his soul and to preach. I remarked that as he was a daily communicant along with my mother, the Lord he met day after day in the Blessed Sacrament would be the same good Lord he'd meet face to face after death. It would be a meeting of friends, not strangers. This is why a worthy reception of Our Lord in Holy Communion is a pledge of future glory.

Suggested resolution: to pray for the Holy Souls in Purgatory at Sunday Mass.

Part Three:
Practical Day-to-Day Needs

Holy Hour - The Mass and the Life of Christ

For this section, I want simply to offer you, dear reader and retreatant, the first paragraph written by Knox for your edification. It is so clear and beautiful that it deserves to be quoted in full:

Our Lord's earthly life divides itself naturally into four periods, differing very much in length, sharply marked off one from another by the changed conditions under which they were lived. First, his birth and the thirty years of obscurity; then the three years or a little less of his public ministry; then the week or if you will the three hours of his Passion; then the forty days of his Risen Life before the Ascension. I don't think it altogether fanciful to see the same fourfold division in that effectual drama which perpetuates his Eucharistic life, the Holy Mass. Leaving out those parts of it which are variable, you can see in the priest's attitude during the early part of the Mass a mirror of the humiliation, the self-annihilation, which belongs to Our Lord's infancy; in his attitude at the offertory, a mirror of the self-oblation which was Our Lord's public life; in his attitude during the canon, a mirror of the self-sacrifice which inspired Our Lord's

Passion; in his attitude during Communion, perhaps less clearly recognisable, a mirror of the glory which shines out from Our Lord's Risen Body, and from its acts.

▶ 17. The Second Conversion

"And the Lord turned and looked straight at Peter." (*Lk* 22:61)

St Peter, the Prince of the Apostles and first pope, experienced, according to Knox, a "second conversion", by Our Lord's tender gaze. Only the evangelist, St Luke, tells us that Jesus turned around and looked at Peter on the occasion of his third denial. St Peter's first conversion was when Our Lord called him to leave his nets and follow him; that made a Christian of him. The third conversion was the day of Pentecost, the Descent of God the Holy Spirit. That made a saint of him, Knox believes. Between these two, spiritual authors call it, "the second conversion".

Knox points out that most conversions differ from the Protestant idea of a sudden event, "which knocks you over like a sledge hammer." For many of us, conversion is a gradual weaning away of the soul from worldliness to God. This gradual movement, evaluated best in spiritual direction with a good and sound guide, occurs by God's gentle and provident care, like a "twitch upon the thread", the title of Book Three in Evelyn Waugh's *Brideshead Revisited*. Conversion, more dynamic than static, means turning or re-orientating. In what direction? Our Lord speaks of being converted and becoming like little children, vulnerable and dependent. Have you ever loved truly by shedding the props and trappings of invulnerability?

We need to move beyond our self-made and membrane-thin sophistication if we desire authentic conversion in order to see things properly under the banner of eternity. St Philip Neri, that wise priest of Renaissance Rome, would challenge the many schemes we concoct by saying as he did to the young man who thought worldly success was enough: "Yes, and then?" We eventually run out of answers of a temporal nature to this pertinent question. May we pray for ourselves and one another that we may hear and heed the voice of the Good Shepherd, on the road of life, on the road of conversion.

Suggested resolution: to consider obtaining a spiritual director.

▶ 18. The Use of God's Creatures

"No one can be the slave of two masters." (Mt 6:24)

No retreat would be complete without a mention of mortification. It is good to ask ourselves from time to time: are we capable in a world of overwhelming choice and opportunity to say: "No" to ourselves? There are, Knox says, two types of mortification: voluntary and involuntary.

The latter type is the better of the two since it is God who arranges things, not me. In the concrete, rather than theoretical discussion, how do we see and use creatures? One way is by means of negation, denying oneself, "offering up", rooting out certain goods, like weeds, so as to leave more room for the love of God to grow more freely in us. The other is the way of affirmation, accepting all that God gives us, the innocent pleasures, to raise our souls up to God. In this particular case, we have to be on guard against selfishness, making sure that this or that enjoyment does not bring with it the occasion of sin.

In classic Knox we are told: after all isn't it rather inconsistent to say thank you to God for his gifts and then tell him that we don't want them? Isn't it a poor compliment to the goodness of the Creator to regard his creatures as something evil? Throughout Christian history, asceticism has taken many forms. Ask some Father of the Desert why he liked such an uncomfortable life and he would have told you: "I must get solitude, I must get silence; my soul has no room to breathe in the heavy atmosphere of the world."

Knox provides a couple of practical suggestions in the way of affirmation. First, do let us get more into the habit of thanking God for things. And especially for plain, simple things which we enjoy almost without knowing it; things like sandwiches on the train and putting on soft shoes after a hard day on your feet. Second, accepting the hospitality of others. You must be very far on in the state of union with God before you dare refuse a present of home grown peas from the man next door. There's a very deep-seated and very silly kind of pride in us which makes us want to say: "No thank you" when offered the loan of an umbrella.

A few rules about the way of negation. First, if your doctor told you that you had only six months more to live, what change would you be introducing into your way of living? Second, take concrete steps, with the view of permanence, to help quit occasions of sin. If you are given to uncharitable talk, for instance, the right mortification for you is silence. Be practical: don't aspire to become the sort of "piebald saint" who sleeps on a board and is not on speaking terms with his sister-in-law. Third, watch your prayer. Are your amusements interfering with your prayer? Make sure that you are not so ordering your life so as to keep God at arm's length. Fourth, do your job well. This is the way of the Christian. We have to do our bit in whatever corner of the Lord's vineyard we find ourselves.

Don't follow the way of affirmation to make people think Christians are superficial or negative to make others think: "How depressing Christians are!" Keep, rather, Knox concludes, "your hand always lying light on the tiller ready to catch any breath of guidance that God will send you."

Suggested resolution: to be silent the next opportunity when you could speak well of yourself.

► 19. On Good Nature

> *"Take the plank out of your own eye first, and then
> you will see clearly enough to take the splinter out
> of your brother's eye."* (Mt 7:5)

We speak of certain of our friends as good natured.
What do we mean by this? Theologically speaking,
it is of course, says Knox, inaccurate, even heretical. The
good-natured people who have lived in the world can be
counted on the fingers of one hand: Our Lady, St John
the Baptist and possibly Jeremiah. Knox does not discuss
here in any explicit way the dogma of the Immaculate
Conception and how Our Lady is truly and unambiguously
"good-natured", being free from the original sin. Rather, he
shifts the emphasis to the importance for us all of doing
things with purity of intention.

On the first Sunday of Advent of 2011, Roman Catholics
in the English speaking world received a new translation of
the Ordinary and Propers of the Mass. Someone gave me
a beautifully made *Daily Roman Missal* and in the section,
"Prayers and Devotions", there is what is called a "Spiritual
Game Plan". In the category of things a Catholic *always*
must do we read: "Do everything for the love of God: this
is *purity of intention*. Always purify your intention. Make
acts of contrition and atonement for your sins and the sins
of others."

Knox produces another gem on this subject that is well
worth quoting:

I am sure you have all read before now the kind of pious book which has a whole chapter, at the very least, on the subject of intention. Most of our actions, when all is said and done, are of themselves indifferent; brushing your hair, or reading a novel, or playing a round of golf, isn't something right or wrong. Has it, therefore, no value? On the contrary, say the spiritual authors, every action has a moral value; it depends on the intention with which it is performed. Brushing your hair out of mere vanity is wrong; reading a novel out of mere curiosity is at the best a waste of time; playing golf in order to boast afterwards about how well you putted is sinful pride. All these things, daily actions that have to be got through, harmless recreations which make us come back to our work with more zest, are good actions if they are performed consciously, to the glory of Almighty God.

Suggested resolution: to make an act of contrition for the lack of purity of intention.

▶ 20. On Minor Trials

"Gather up the broken pieces that are left over, so that nothing may be wasted." (Jn 6:12)

Knox says he is surprised by the words of Our Lord after the feeding of the five thousand, "Gather up the broken pieces that are left over, so that nothing may be wasted."

How is it that God-made-man is interested in detail like this? Do we not at times wonder in our lives if the Lord is interested in us, our problems, our broken hearts? How can the Word through whom and by whom everything was made care about the "smallness" in our lives?

It is important to return to the Incarnation and see that God is not distant, but close, near and accessible. He is Emmanuel: God-with-us. As Pope Benedict XVI said reassuringly in his encyclical on Christian hope, *Spe Salvi*: "When no one listens to me any more, God still listens to me." What is significant to me, is not insignificant to Christ our Intercessor before our Heavenly Father. The "broken pieces" of our lives, disappointments, failed love, setbacks, yes all these and more, are important to the Lord because they mean something to us. Our Lord's Sacred Heart is our refuge: he desires to comfort us, to give us rest. Our Lord sends us others to help and to inspire us along the way.

Knox says:

It is at such times of disillusionment that we can comfort ourselves with his words, "Gather up the broken pieces that are left over, so that nothing may be wasted." He, with all the economy of a universe passing between his hands, is not too busy to look after the scraps. And indeed, for fear we should be blind to that, for fear we should lose sight of that, he has given us a saint in our own times whose characteristic message is that a lifetime of small endurances may, through his grace and Providence, be a life of exceptional achievement. That is the revelation which makes St Theresa of Lisieux still, in the best sense, popular. It is not a question of miracles; it is not a question of gaudy statues and pretty-pretty devotions. The reason why people still listen to St Theresa of Lisieux is because she taught us that heroic sanctity does not mean, necessarily, doing heroic things.

Suggested resolution: to be attentive to the reality of wastefulness, for example, at meal times, and resolve to change. Or, make an offering to the poor through the St Vincent de Paul Society.

▶ 21. Liberty of the Spirit in Prayer

"Lord, teach us to pray." (*Lk* 11:1)

The best way to pray is to pray as you can. This is the essence of what Knox calls the "liberty of the spirit in prayer." Our prayers need to be our own prayers, not some form of mimicry, however attractive this may be to us at first. Prayer means talking and listening to God. Knox asks us to think of a father who has come home with a present for his little son, knowing that it is what his son wants, but waiting for it to be asked for it. It is simple really, and we complicate things, don't we? We think it ought to be an uncomfortable or complex business. We are to go to him easily and naturally, like children.

When Adam and Eve were tossed out of Paradise, the first thing they noticed, says Knox, that had gone wrong was that they had distractions in their prayer. They had never had those before. Ever since then we too have suffered what appears to be a losing battle against distraction. St Francis de Sales is wise on the subject: if we find we pray best lying down, it is our job to pray lying down. For public prayer, that is, Mass on Sundays and holidays, Knox states that the first thing is to be present. So much more follows from simply "showing up".

It was said of St Francis of Assisi that if you asked him to pray for you, he knelt down and did it there and then. We should be regular in our prayers but not rule out spontaneity, to "strike out a little". God wants us to be ourselves, to go to him as our Father, "not to treat him as if we were trying to put across a difficult message to someone who was rather deaf and rather stupid." We are to use simple language or just be quiet in the warmth of his presence.

Knox recommends the Holy Rosary (the subject of the next chapter) - a weapon of prayer, common to all sorts and unites you with your Catholic friends everywhere, with prisoners, with the sick; it is mainstream Catholic life. "God wants us to use the liberty of the spirit, and come to him boldly", Knox concludes, "as his children, choosing the prayer that suits us best."

Suggested resolution: to pray for the intentions of the Holy Father.

▶ 22. The Holy Rosary

"The Word was made flesh, he lived among us... full of grace and truth." (Jn 1:14)

Knox could not have envisioned the addition of the Mysteries of Light and so these are not treated in this section. Knox uses a rather charming phrase to describe the Holy Rosary which he calls "the furniture of our lives as Catholics". As such, we can take it too much for granted, perhaps like the sofa in our living room. It is the sort of devotion, he says, which causes us more scruples when we forget to say it than comfort us when we remember.

The Holy Rosary has its own feast (7th October) to remind us of its meaning. It is the only inanimate thing, save the holy cross and the chair of St Peter, which has a feast in the Universal Calendar.

Here are some aspects of the Holy Rosary for your consideration. First, it is a source of meditation. As the beads occupy our fingers, the prayers are to occupy our minds, and leave our minds free to meditate. Second, the Rosary can be said in private or public, and it links us the world over. Third, the Dominican Order was used to spread the devotion to combat the heresies of mediaeval Europe, by highlighting the Incarnation. It is indeed Our Lady's Rosary, but it is the life of her Divine Son that we are to think about especially. If we believe in the Incarnation, of God's closeness to us, how can we be but close to our neighbour wherever we find ourselves? Our Lord's Incarnation links the beads together.

Knox says that we think of the Holy Rosary as a "musical composition in three moods": Joyful, Sorrowful and Glorious. Joyful, because the birth of Our Lord is the climax. Sorrowful, clearly because of the death and crucifixion of the Lord and Glorious (the triumph over death), where eternity wins out - "man delivered at last from this patchwork alternation of joy and sorrow, and finding his true medium at last in the endless contemplation of God."

Knox rounds off this moving chapter by saying this: "He brought joy with him into the world, and brought it first of all to her, to whom it belonged as a right because she was his mother." *May he, whose only begotten Son by his life, death and Resurrection has purchased the rewards of eternal life, grant that we, meditating on these mysteries with the most Holy Rosary of the Blessed Virgin Mary, may both imitate what they contain and obtain what they promise. Amen.*

Suggested resolution: to pray a decade of the Rosary this evening.

▶ 23. St Mary Magdalene

"I have called you friends, because I have made known to you everything I have learnt from my Father." (Jn 15:15)

Knox calls St Mary Magdalene, a friend of the Lord, whose life needs little in the way of "rhetorical embroidery", a heroine of contrition, of resignation and of hope. After the death of Christ, she desires to find him still, to anoint his Body, as a token of her love. Her love for the Lord is inspiring and real, because she was loved by him first. She is able to give what she first received.

In this section I would like to touch briefly on the subject of friendship as one cannot help but think of this when one considers Our Lord and St Mary Magdalene. Cicero, as is often quoted, called a friend, "another self". In the book of *Sirach*, we read that a faithful friend is a "sturdy shelter" and a "treasure". Our Lord himself refers to those in his inner circle as "friends" and "servants no longer".

When I was in the seminary in Toronto I had a superb priest-spiritual director, an Oblate of St Francis de Sales, who taught me a beautiful scheme for understanding the nature of friendship and a way by which to assess whether friendships are authentic or simply acquaintances. He said there are four stages to consider: attraction, eating together, sharing a common endeavour and revealing a secret or mystery of oneself. These four, though first appearing in the aforementioned order, become more fluid with maturation.

The four stages of friendship were evident in Our Lord's life with his friends: the disciples followed him, being drawn and attracted to him first; they ate together many times, before and after the Resurrection, and particularly in the Last Supper; how often they prayed together, rested, walked, fished; finally, Our Lord told them the message of his parables and who he was: God's own Son, the long-awaited Messiah.

Let us take this time as an opportunity to pray for our friends, and pray for those who are lonely. May our faith make us always more personal as we seek to draw more and more souls into friendship with Christ who will never let us down, who never tires of us, who is not embarrassed by us, who loves us in ways we can barely fathom. St Mary Magdalene, *pray for us*.

Suggested resolution: to contact a housebound relative or friend.

▶ 24. Our Lady's Serenity

"My soul proclaims the greatness of the Lord, and my spirit exalts in God my Saviour." (Lk 1:46-47)

The last section of this helpful book by Knox concentrates our minds on Our Lady. It is traditional to end sermons and homilies with a reference to Our Lady, asking for her maternal solicitude and heavenly aid. This can be seen in many of the addresses and writings of the Roman pontiffs down through the ages. And I shall follow this tradition, thus concluding our retreat.

Knox presents what he calls a "human picture" of Our Lady, drawn from the Gospels. It is possible to forget, on account of the artistic renderings of Our Lady we see on our classical Christmas cards, drawn from Gentile models, that Our Lady was Jewish. We may rightly picture her with a jug of water on her shoulders. She talked, like St Peter, with a "bit of a Galilean brogue".

Knox does not desire to focus on the stuff of biographies, but on the one quality called "serenity". He thinks of serenity as a "human quality, reacting to human situations," to imagine the smile…which "lingered on her face and threw into relief the thoughtfulness of her brow." It is a useful quality to remember in Our Lady, and we all need it. The great calmness of Our Lady is something for us to call to mind. We see it in these ways:

• At the Annunciation, though bewildered, she listened. She pondered. She simply says: "Yes, but how?"

• At the Visitation, Our Lady arose with haste, not hurry, to greet her cousin, Elizabeth. "Calm people don't need to be in a hurry, because they hasten at the right moment, about the right things."

• In the *Magnificat*, while she starts with herself, she moves away from the subject as soon as possible, to focus on the goodness of God and certain other generalities.

• In Bethlehem, we read: "*And* she wrapped him in his swaddling clothes *and* she laid him in a manger." The "ands", Knox says, are there to show that Our Lady simply got on with things as they needed to be done - no fuss, no running around in circles because the inn was full. "I don't see any reason to doubt", says Knox, "that St Luke got his Gospel of the Infancy from Our Lady herself." Can't you hear Our Lady describing the scene to him: "It was so convenient, really, with all the straw about; and very quiet, you know."

• At Cana, her advice is calm and measured, not panicky and verbose. "Do whatever he tells you." It was the motto of Our Lady's life.

A few resolutions, then, are in order:

• Make haste in life, and do something good for others, as an "antidote against unprofitable day-dreaming."

• Do make the best of what comes, remember that tragedy will visit us and, importantly, will *leave* us too.

• Trust in God - sometimes we are anxious - don't be! Leave things in the hands of God, very quietly, very serenely.

Knox concludes this last section and his book with a salute to the Mother of God and our Mother too, given us at the foot of the cross:

It is not easy advice that she gives, and we must certainly have recourse to her if we are to win the grace to carry it out. Let us leave it in her hands, then, to advise us and to help us carry out her advice; let us go to her with our troubles, our faults, our inadequacies, and put them in her hands, confident that her serene competence will know how to deal with them. She will not fail us; she has a mother's wisdom, and a mother's love.

Suggested resolution: to pray a Hail Mary thanking Our Lady for aiding you during this time of reflection/retreat.

Ronald Knox

Ronald Arbuthnott Knox was born in Leicestershire, England, in 1888. The son of an Anglican bishop, he attended Oxford and quickly established a reputation for scholarship. Influenced by the writings of Robert Hugh Benson, he became an Anglican minister in 1912, though the path to Rome would not be long in coming.

By the time he entered the Church in 1917, Knox had already established himself as a capable apologist for the faith. Though influenced by G.K. Chesterton, the younger Knox would later influence Chesterton to enter the Catholic Church in 1922.

Knox was appointed the chaplain of the Catholic students at Oxford where he continued to write. Among some of his works were satires and detective stories.

With the outbreak of World War II, Knox found himself in great demand as a radio personality. He also unexpectedly became the chaplain at a school for Catholic girls. In 1939, Knox began a nine-year project which resulted in a new English translation of the Bible. It was one of his last works, *Enthusiasm* (1950), which Knox himself regarded as his greatest.

A world of Catholic reading at your fingertips...

Catholic Faith, Life & Truth for all

CTS
www.CTSbooks.org

twitter: @CTSpublishers

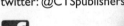

facebook.com/CTSpublishers

Catholic Truth Society, Publishers to the Holy See.